40-DAY DEVOTIONAL JOURNEY

MADE

IN

THE

MIDDLE

MYRAIO L. MITCHELL, SR.

BECAUSE THERE'S MORE PUBLISHING | GEORGIA

ISBN: 979-8-9921977-0-9 (Hardback)
ISBN: 979-8-9921977-1-6 (Paperback)

Library of Congress Control Number: 2025902830

Printed in the United States of America.

Published by:
Because There's More Publishing LLC
PO Box 390163
Snellville, GA 30039
becausetheresmorepublishing.com

CONTENTS

INTRODUCTION

I was recently asked why I decided to write this book of devotions, and I think this is a great question. Before I answer, let me first say thank you for your support by partnering with me in sharing this journey with others.

So, why did I write this book of devotions?

Through the years, I have been blessed to serve alongside some renowned leaders in both the marketplace and in ministry. During this journey, life was unfolding all around me sometimes because of my own choices, and other times because change was simply inevitable. I married young and started a family, raising two beautiful daughters and a son, then found myself going through a divorce. I transitioned from one job to another, while also grieving the loss of my mother to brain cancer. Years later, I remarried, and we now have two more beautiful daughters, making me a parent to five amazing children. Life happened fast and often felt out of control.

In the midst of raising a blended family, I also faced bankruptcy - not because I had been careless with resources, but because I felt God calling me to leave a 16-year corporate career to follow His path for me. My "release scripture" in this season was Isaiah 41:10-13 AMP:

"Do not fear [anything], for I am with you; Do not be afraid, for I am your God. I will strengthen you, be assured I will help you; I will certainly take hold of you with My righteous right hand [a hand of justice, of power, of victory, of salvation]. Indeed, all those who are angry with you will be put to shame and humiliated; Those who strive against you will be as nothing and will perish. You shall search for those who quarrel with you, but will not find them; They who war against you will be as nothing, as nothing at all. For I, the Lord your God, keep hold of your right hand; [I am the Lord], Who says to you, 'Do not fear, I will help you.'"

By faith, I resigned to pursue my passion for ministry. I didn't have another job lined up, and my income dropped drastically, from six figures to $20,000 a year. This leap of faith was just the beginning of even greater challenges. During this time, my brother died, and my father's words to me were, "Take care of it." A few years later, I received a call that no one ever wants - my father had passed away. Eighteen months later, while working, I received another call that my sister had died. She and I had spoken just 12 hours earlier. She was unmarried and had no children, and I could almost hear my father's voice again, saying, "Take care of it."

Looking back over the last 30 years, I believe that nothing just happens. Every situation, trial, mountain-top and valley-low experience, disappointment, and even the mistakes have been part of a greater plan. It is by His grace that things turned around for my good. I now understand that I was being "Made in the Middle" - the place between the promise and its fulfillment. And I still am and so are you.

Know you are exactly where you need to be to become the best version of yourself - not what others expect, but who God created you to be.

Blessings,
Myraio

GOD'S NAME IS ON IT

Most manufactured products come with warranties or guarantees, and the strength of that warranty often depends on the credibility of the manufacturer's name. If a company's reputation is strong, customers are more inclined to trust that the manufacturer will deliver on its promises. How much more, then, should we believe and trust our Heavenly Father to fulfill His Word?

Unlike human enterprises, God will never go out of business. He is eternal, unchanging, and unfailing. God stands watch over His Word, ensuring every promise He has made is fulfilled (Jer. 1:12). He never overpromises or underdelivers. With God, there are no limitations, and nothing is impossible (Mt. 19:26). His Word is trustworthy, backed by the full honor of His name (Ps. 138:2). You can take God at His Word - His name is on it!

DAY 1

I bow before your holy Temple as I worship. I praise your name for your unfailing love and faithfulness; for your promises are backed by all the honor of your name.

Psalm 138:2 NLT

Reflection: What promises has God made to you? Write them out, and after each one, record: "God's name is on it."

_____

_____

_____

_____

_____

_____

_____

_____

_____

_____

_____

_____

_____

_____

_____

_____

_____

_____

_____

_____

_____

_____

GOD CANNOT LIE

God is not a human who lies or a mortal who changes his mind. When he says something, he will do it; when he makes a promise, he will fulfill it.

Numbers 23:19 CJB

Imagine trusting someone who never breaks a promise, never wavers, and whose every word is absolutely true. In a world where promises can be empty and words don't always align with actions, this level of trustworthiness is hard to fathom. But with God, it's a cast-iron certainty.

You will never see an eagle playing tennis, a fish performing a piano recital, or a lion driving a car. Why? Because these actions are impossible for them - they go against their very nature. Similarly, God's nature makes it impossible for Him to lie. Just as absurd as it is to imagine a lion driving a car, so it is to imagine God being anything but truthful. Lying is simply not in His DNA.

The purpose of a lie is to deceive, but God has no need to deceive us. Unlike Satan - the father of lies, who introduced

DAY

2

He has given us both his promise and his oath, two things we can completely count on, for it is impossible for God to tell a lie.

Hebrews 6:18 TLB

doubt and deception in the Garden, God is the source of all truth. Every word He speaks, He fulfills, and every promise He makes, He keeps. He does not change, waver, or falter.

When God speaks, you can trust that His Word is as solid as His nature. Stand confidently in His promises, knowing He will do exactly what He has said.

Reflection: How might your life change, if you fully embraced the truth that God cannot lie? In what areas of your life do you need to lean more confidently on God's unchanging Word?

_____

_____

_____

_____

_____

_____

_____

_____

_____

_____

_____

_____

_____

GOD'S WORD WILL PRODUCE

"As the rain and snow come down from heaven and stay upon the ground to water the earth, and cause the grain to grow and to produce seed for the farmer and bread for the hungry, so also is my word. I send it out, and it always produces fruit. It shall accomplish all I want it to and prosper everywhere I send it."
Isaiah 55:10-11 TLB

A farmer plants seeds expecting it to yield a crop. A fisherman drops his net, expecting to yield a catch. But when God speaks His Word, He doesn't merely hope His Word will accomplish its purpose - He knows it will. Every word He speaks is infused with His power; set in motion to produce exactly what He intended.

When God declared His Word over you, He wasn't merely hoping it would produce. He knew it would not return to Him void of its purpose. Even now, you can look around and still see God's Word manifesting what He spoke in Genesis through Revelations. Thousands of years later, what He spoke is still bearing fruit.

DAY 3

Ah, Lord God! Behold, You have made the heavens and the earth by Your great power and outstretched arm. There is nothing too hard for You.
Jeremiah 32:17 NKJV

15

If you find yourself in the "middle," waiting for what God has spoken to fully unfold, remember that the process doesn't diminish His power. His Word is still at work, right here and now, producing exactly what He intended. Stand firm in faith, knowing that God's Word will accomplish what He promised.

Reflection: Take a moment to reflect on what God has already done for you. What fruit has He already manifested in your life? What fruit is He producing within you? Let this serve as your personal reminder that God's Word will produce!

_____

_____

_____

_____

_____

_____

_____

_____

_____

_____

_____

_____

_____

_____

YES AND AMEN

"For no matter how many promises God has made,
they are "Yes" in Christ. And so through Him the "Amen"
is spoken by us to the glory of God."
2 Corinthians 1:20 NIV

When God makes a promise, it's final. He doesn't waver, hesitate, or change His mind. His promises are more than just words - they are unshakable, trustworthy, and certain. Every promise He makes finds its "Yes" in Christ, affirming that His Word will stand. Because of this, you never have to wonder if God will fulfill what He has spoken over your life; from the moment He declared it, He already deemed you worthy of receiving it.

The "Amen" is your response to God's promise. It is your personal "Yes" to what He has declared, an affirmation that you believe His Word is true and that He is faithful to fulfill it. In saying "Amen," you are standing in agreement with God, declaring, "So let it be." Hold tightly to your "Yes," because God will never let go of His.

DAY

4

*Let us hold fast the confession of
our hope without wavering, for He
who promised is faithful.*
Hebrews 10:23 NKJV

Reflection: Is your 'Yes' still intact? If not, how can you realign your heart with His will and offer Him your 'Yes' once again?

Practical Application

1. **Anchor Yourself in God's Promises**: Write down promises that resonate with your current season and keep them where you can see them daily.
2. **Declare "Amen" in Faith**: Respond to God's promises with your own "Amen." Whenever doubt arises, reaffirm your belief by declaring that God's Word will produce what He intends.
3. **Expect Fruitful Results in God's Timing**: Stay patient, knowing that His Word will accomplish everything He sent it to do.

Affirmation

I will stand strong and remain at peace, trusting the Lord to sustain me. Father, Your promises are yes and amen, and I refuse anything that hinders Your provision for my life and my family. I declare courage and faith, knowing You are with me. All spiritual hindrances are bound, and Your promises prevail. I walk in peace and strength, trusting in Your faithfulness.

PROMISE PREREQUISITES
IT'S NOT ALL ON GOD

How many times have you said or heard the words, "I'm waiting on God?" We often say this when we're in the "middle" - the space between God's promise and its fulfillment. In this place, we're hoping and trusting that His Word will manifest in our lives. And rest assured, God is faithful to His promises!

However, today I encourage you to pause and consider: Could God be waiting on you?

There are moments when, rather than us waiting on God, He is waiting for us. Perhaps He is looking for a response, an act of faith, or a heart fully surrendered to His will. Sometimes, whether it's a tangible step or an internal shift, He asks us to move first.

DAY 5

But seek first the kingdom of God and His righteousness, and all these things shall be added to you.

Matthew 6:33 NKJV

1. **Believe** – God may be waiting for you to truly believe what He has spoken - not just as a vague hope, but as a firm conviction that His promise is meant for you personally. He wants your heart anchored in His Word.
2. **Obedience** – Sometimes, God is waiting for that first step of obedience. Faith requires action. Yes, His instructions may challenge you, but trust that He sees the bigger picture. What are you doing to prepare for His promise? If He has promised you a new home, are you getting ready for it? If He has promised you a spouse, are you preparing your heart and life for that relationship? If He has promised you freedom from debt, how are you stewarding your resources?
3. **Trust** - Life's challenges may cause you to question what God said, but remember: your current circumstances do not cancel God's promise. Trust that He is greater than any obstacle, and that He will fulfill what He said.

Before placing it all on God, take a moment to reflect: Is there something He is waiting on from you? When you have met the prerequisites for the promise, you'll see its fulfillment - **GUARANTEED!** His Word will not return void; it will accomplish the purpose for which it was sent (Isaiah 55:11).

Reflection: In what ways could your action or inaction impact the fulfillment of God's promises in your life?

_____

_____

_____

_____

_____

_____

_____

_____

_____

_____

_____

_____

_____

_____

_____

_____

_____

_____

_____

_____

COLLABORATIVE FAITH PARTNER

"Now faith is the substance of things hoped for,
the evidence of things not seen."
Hebrews 11:1 NKJV

When we think of a collaborative partner, it's often from a business perspective - individuals or entities joining forces to accomplish a specific goal. These partnerships are common in the marketplace. But have you ever considered that God is calling you into a collaborative partnership with Him - a relationship where you enter into an agreement, working in sync with His plan for your life to accomplish His will on earth?

We are God's Collaborative Faith Partners! "Collaborative" because we work with Him, not against Him. This partnership requires faith - faith to respond, faith to agree with His plans, and faith to step into the role He's called you to. And "partner" because we are the ones He chooses to execute His will. God has entrusted each of us with specific assignments to further His purposes.

DAY

6

Work out your own salvation with fear and trembling; for it is God who works in you both to will and to do for His good pleasure.
Philippians 2:12-13 NKJV

26

Now is the time to wholeheartedly embrace your relationship with God and the collaborative journey He has laid out for your life. He knew exactly who you were when He selected you for the assignment. He deemed you worthy and capable in Him. Your willingness to join forces with God may be the very vehicle that leads you to the promise He has prepared for you.

Reflection: Are you ready to fully embrace your role as God's collaborative partner? What steps of faith is He asking you to take today in alignment with His will?

_____

_____

_____

_____

_____

_____

_____

_____

_____

_____

_____

_____

_____

_____

WILLING AND OBEDIENT

"If you are willing and obedient,
you shall eat the good of the land."
Isaiah 1:19 NKJV

Are you willing? And next, are you obedient? One of the greatest barriers to walking in God's promises is not usually our willingness; we often have that part covered. The real challenge lies in the follow-through - our obedience to what God has spoken and the instructions He's given.

Isaiah 1:19 reminds us: "If you are willing and obedient, you shall eat the good of the land." Willingness alone, while admirable, is not enough. Both willingness and obedience are essential to unlocking certain promises. They are part of the prerequisites for stepping into the fullness of what God has prepared.

Yes, God knows the intentions of our hearts, and He is always ready to give us strength when we cry out for help. But let's be honest, obedience often comes at a cost. It might mean letting go of something we hold dear, walking away

DAY

7

Listen! Obedience is better than sacrifice, and submission is better than offering the fat of rams.
1 Samuel 15:22 NLT

from certain relationships or surrendering our own desires. Obedience can stretch us, pushing us beyond what's familiar or comfortable.

Yet, instead of focusing on what obedience will cost you, reflect on what your obedience will allow you to gain. What blessings await on the other side of your "Yes" to God? And consider this: what is the cost of disobedience? What are you missing by holding back? The temporary discomfort or sacrifice pales in comparison to the promises that will be fulfilled and the glory that God will reveal in your life.

Reflection: Are you simply willing, or are you following through in obedience? What might God be asking you to surrender or step into today to experience His promises?

_____

_____

_____

_____

_____

_____

_____

_____

_____

_____

TRUST GOD WITH THE PROMISE

"Do not let this happy trust in the Lord die away, no matter
what happens. Remember your reward!"
Hebrews 10:35 TLB

TRUST - a five-letter word whose substance is weightier
than gold. Merrian Webster defines trust as *an assured
reliance on the character, ability, strength, or truth of
someone or something.* When we say we trust God, we are
declaring that He is and not only that, but He is reliable, He
is truth, He is able, and He is strong. Life's challenges -
situations and circumstances - do not alter or diminish the
truth of who God is. He remains unchanging in His nature,
regardless of what we face.

When we reflect on His unchangingness, we can trust God
with the promise, even when times seem unfavorable. When
the storms of life rage, and when circumstances appear to
contradict what God has spoken, it's easy to lose heart. The
"middle" can present numerous opportunities to cast aside
our confidence. But we must hold fast to the faithfulness and
nature of the One who made the promise. He is bigger than

DAY
8

*Trust in the Lord with all your heart,
and lean not on your own understanding;
in all your ways acknowledge Him,
and He shall direct your paths.*

Proverbs 3:5-6 NKJV

our storms. He is greater than our doubts. He is all powerful and thus can fulfill every word. Nothing is impossible for Him. You can trust God with the promise.

Reflection: Where in your life is God asking you to trust Him more deeply? What circumstances are tempting you to doubt His faithfulness?

_____

_____

_____

_____

_____

_____

_____

_____

_____

_____

_____

_____

_____

_____

_____

_____

Practical Application

1. **Write Down the Attributes of God's Nature:** Spend a few moments listing qualities of God. Reflect on His promises with the understanding of who He is. How does His character assure you that He will fulfill what He's spoken? Let this understanding deepen your trust and confidence in His timing and plans.
2. **Identify One Act of Faith:** Choose one practical step that aligns with the promise you're waiting on. For example, if you're waiting for a financial breakthrough, decide on one positive financial habit you can start today.
3. **Pray**: Pray and ask God to reveal any areas where you may need to grow in belief, obedience, or trust. Ask Him to help you recognize and act on any specific steps He's prompting you to take. Make it a point to listen for His guidance each day and be willing to move forward when He nudges you.

Affirmation

Today, I take responsibility for my life and commit to changing its trajectory. I will be intentional with my time, talents, and treasures, knowing I have what it takes to succeed. I thank You, Father, for growing my faith and teaching me to trust You. I stand strong, firm, and confident, trusting You to meet my needs and guide me through every challenge.

THE PROCESS OF CHANGE IN THE DARKROOM

The process of change in the darkroom is much like developing film. In photography, a darkroom is a special environment where light-sensitive photographic paper is carefully exposed to light in a controlled way. One process that is used is called "Red Lighting." This allows the photographer to develop the image without destroying it. Without this careful process, a photograph can be prematurely exposed and ruined, never reaching its full potential.

Similarly, when we resist the process of change that God is calling us to, we risk exposing ourselves too soon - stepping into places we're not yet prepared for. This can distort the image of who God created us to be.

DAY 9

Early in the morning, while it was still dark, Jesus got up, left [the house], and went out to a secluded place, and was praying there.

Mark 1:35 AMP

Often, it's not others who expose or derail us. Many times, it's our own impatience. By stepping out before God has fully equipped us, we limit His work in us.

The process of change in the darkroom requires us to:

- **Engage with God**: Stay connected to Him in prayer and through a personal relationship.
- **Be Equipped by God**: Allow Him to prepare us for the call and purpose on our lives.
- **Be Empowered by God**: Receive His anointing and favor to walk in the purpose He has given us.

When we admire athletes, innovators, or public figures, we celebrate the end result, but we rarely see the process behind their glory - the sweat, the tears, the struggles. Even Jesus spent time alone in His own "darkroom," Gethsemane, where He prayed and prepared for His greatest purpose (Matthew 26:36).

At some point, each of us will enter our own darkroom - a sacred space with God. In the stillness, free from distractions, we can truly hear His voice and be shaped by His hand. You are never alone there; God is with you, carefully molding and preparing you for what's next. Though it may feel isolating, this hidden place is where you're equipped for the destiny He has planned. Just as a beautiful photograph emerges from the darkroom only after a careful process, so too does God bring forth beauty in us through these times of preparation.

Reflection: Are there areas in your life where you might be stepping out prematurely? How can you lean into God's "darkroom" process, trusting Him to equip and prepare you fully before you move forward?

_____

_____

_____

_____

_____

_____

_____

_____

_____

_____

_____

_____

_____

_____

_____

_____

_____

_____

CALLED TO SEPARATE

"Now the Lord had said to Abram: "Get out of your country, From your family and from your father's house, To a land that I will show you."
Genesis 12:1 NKJV

Abraham's journey began with a call to leave behind everything familiar - his country, his people, and his family. This act of separation was the first step in God's plan to make Abraham the father of many nations. By stepping out in faith, Abraham embarked on a journey of complete dependence on God. In this separation, God set him apart for a purpose far greater than he could have imagined.

Sometimes, God calls us to leave behind what feels safe and comfortable. This may include relationships, places, or familiar routines. Separation can be painful, but it is often necessary for growth. When God asks us to let go, He is making space to bless us in ways that only He can. By trusting Him, we open ourselves to His greater purpose.

DAY
10

Fear of man will prove to be a snare, but whoever trusts in the LORD is kept safe.
Proverbs 29:25 NIV

Reflection: How has God used seasons of separation in your life to deepen your reliance on Him? Where might God be calling you to separate from what's familiar or comfortable? Do you trust that God's purpose in separation is for your good, even if it's difficult to see right now?

CALLED TO SOLITUDE

"So He Himself often withdrew
into the wilderness and prayed."
Luke 5:16 NKJV

In seasons when life feels stagnant or we face delays and disappointments, it's easy to question our purpose. But waiting doesn't mean our destiny has changed. Often, God uses solitude to reframe our focus, allowing us to grow closer to Him and hear His voice more clearly. Jesus regularly practiced solitude, prioritizing it even over the demands around Him. For Him, solitude wasn't a luxury; it was essential for staying aligned with His purpose and connected to God's heart.

Consider how Jesus used solitude: to recharge after hard work, prepare for major tasks, grieve, gain wisdom, and make critical decisions. When we feel "stuck" or uncertain, solitude becomes a space where God reminds us that our destiny is secure in Him. In these quiet moments, free from distractions, God reshapes our hearts and refocuses us on the greater purpose He has prepared.

DAY

11

*Be still, and know that I am God; I
will be exalted among the nations, I
will be exalted in the earth!*

Psalm 46:10 NKJV

43

When we embrace solitude as Jesus did, we position ourselves to receive God's perspective and peace, anchoring ourselves in His promises. Trust that He is leading you to fulfill your purpose - even if the path looks different than expected.

Reflection: Could there be areas in your life where God might be inviting you to step into solitude with Him? How can embracing quiet moments help you gain clarity and stay grounded in His purpose?

_____

_____

_____

_____

_____

_____

_____

_____

_____

_____

_____

_____

_____

_____

THE END OF A SEASON

"Moses answered the people, 'Do not be afraid.
Stand firm and you will see the deliverance the Lord will
bring you today. The Egyptians you see today you will
never see again. The Lord will fight for you; you need only
to be still."
Exodus 14:13-14 NIV

Before an image is fully developed in the darkroom, the negative undergoes a careful process, including termination - the removal of elements that would distort or weaken the final image. Similarly, as the Israelites left Egypt, they encountered their own "termination" process: the end of their old life in bondage and the beginning of a new, uncertain journey to freedom. The moment they crossed the Red Sea, they couldn't turn back; that chapter of their life was closed. God used this process to strip away their old identity as slaves, preparing them to live as His chosen people.

In our lives, God often calls us to let go of old habits, relationships, or mindsets that no longer serve His purpose.

DAY

12

To everything there is a season,
A time for every purpose under heaven:
Ecclesiastes 3:1 NIV

This can be painful, especially when we can't yet see what He's preparing us for. But just as the darkroom process refines and clarifies the image, God uses these endings to remove the parts that might distort or weaken His image in us. By letting go, we make room to become and receive the new He has planned.

Maybe God has you in a darkroom season, where He's calling you to release something from the past. It might feel like an ending, but God is using this time to prepare you for what's ahead. Trust Him with the ending of this season and for the opening of your new season.

Reflection: Is there something in your life that God is asking you to release in this darkroom season? How might letting go of the past help you embrace the new things God has for your future?

_____

_____

_____

_____

_____

_____

_____

_____

_____

_____

Practical Application

1. **Identify What Needs Letting Go**: Take time to reflect on areas in your life that may need "termination" for growth to happen. Write down any habits, relationships, mindsets, or routines that no longer align with God's purpose for you.
2. **Set Aside Time for Solitude**: Make a commitment to spend intentional time alone with God each day this week. Let these moments of solitude become spaces where you can pray and listen, free from distractions.
3. **Reflect on Past Seasons**: Consider a past season in your life where you went through significant change or an ending. Reflect on how God used that time to develop you or bring you closer to His purpose. Write down any insights and thank Him for how He has guided you through transitions before. Use these reflections to strengthen your trust in His work in your current season.

Affirmation

Today, I take responsibility for my life and commit to changing its trajectory. I will be intentional with my time, talents, and treasures, knowing I have what it takes to succeed. I thank You, Father, for growing my faith and teaching me to trust You. I stand strong, firm, and confident, trusting You to meet my needs and guide me through every challenge.

GOD'S WAITING ROOM

DAY 13

Just as the darkroom plays a role in God's overall plan for our lives, so does His waiting room. God doesn't waste a moment in our lives. He uses every second for our growth and His glory. This season is an opportunity to draw closer to Him, build our prayer life, and prepare ourselves for the fulfillment of His promises.

Having said that, waiting can be challenging, especially in a culture that's all about speed and instant gratification. Today, we rarely have to wait for anything. We can order what we want and have it within days or even hours. But in God's kingdom, there is purpose in the waiting. He isn't concerned with our timelines but with our growth and maturity. Waiting is one of the ways God develops our character and strengthens our faith.

For you have need of endurance, so that after you have done the will of God, you may receive the promise.

Hebrews 10:36 NKJV

In the first Book of Samuel, chapters 1 and 2, we see Hannah waiting for years to have a child, enduring taunts and heartbreak along the way. Instead of giving up, she held on and endured until God answered. As Hebrews 10:36 says, "For you have need of endurance, so that after you have done the will of God, you may receive the promise." Like Hannah, we sometimes find ourselves in God's waiting room, wondering when He will answer our prayers. In those moments, it's tempting to doubt, rush, or try to make things happen on our own. But God's timing is perfect, even when it seems slow to us. Waiting seasons aren't about delay for delay's sake. He's building us while we wait.

Reflection: What is God asking you to wait on in this season of life? Have you been trying to rush God's timing, or are you allowing Him to work in you as you wait?

_____

_____

_____

_____

_____

_____

_____

_____

_____

_____

THE PLACE OF TRANSFORMATION

"Beloved, now we are children of God;
and it has not yet been revealed what we shall be,
but we know that when He is revealed, we shall be like
Him, for we shall see Him as He is."
1 John 3:2 NKJV

It's in times of waiting that our faith is tested. Just as a child struggles to understand the difference between "not yet" and "no," we, too, can grow impatient, wanting immediate answers. But God sees the full picture, and in His waiting room, He prepares us for what lies ahead. Waiting is not a denial; it's often a necessary place that facilitates our becoming more like Him.

God's waiting room is a place of transformation. God is more interested in who we are becoming than in what we're trying to achieve. In these seasons, God builds our endurance, refines our character, and prepares us for His promises. If you're in His waiting room today, remember: God hasn't forgotten you. He is simply changing you from the inside out for His Glory.

DAY 14

But we all, with unveiled face, beholding as in a mirror the glory of the Lord, are being transformed into the same image from glory to glory, just as by the Spirit of the Lord.

2 Corinthians 3:18 NKJV

Reflection: How might God be using this waiting room season to shape who you're becoming?

_____

_____

_____

_____

_____

_____

_____

_____

_____

_____

_____

_____

_____

_____

_____

_____

_____

_____

_____

_____

_____

A NEW WAY OF THINKING

"Let this mind be in you which was also in Christ Jesus."
Philippians 2:5 NKJV

Change is an essential, often uncomfortable, part of the Christian journey, one that calls us to be transformed from the inside out. In Romans 12:2, Paul encourages us to break free from the patterns of this world by renewing our minds. True transformation begins here, as we align our thoughts with God's, stepping away from frustration and impatience and moving toward a mindset of trust and surrender.

Waiting seasons are often where this renewal happens most profoundly. In God's waiting room, our thoughts are challenged, feelings are stirred, and our patience tested. God uses these times to reshape the way we think. Instead of viewing delays as obstacles, He invites us to see them as fundamental to His plan for our lives. Jesus Himself modeled this mindset of patience, obedience, and humility. In Philippians 2, we see Christ's surrender to God's plan and His trust in God's perfect timing.

DAY 15

And do not be conformed to this world, but be transformed by the renewing of your mind, that you may prove what is that good and acceptable and perfect will of God.

Romans 12:2 NKJV

To embrace the change God calls us into, we need to be willing to renew our minds daily, immersing ourselves in His Word. Letting go of old thought patterns, allows God to shape us more fully into the people He has destined us to be.

Change isn't about temporary shifts but a deeper turning toward God's thoughts and ways. As we trust in His timing and surrender to His process, we open ourselves up to the transformation that aligns us with His "good, pleasing, and perfect will." With renewed minds, we are equipped to navigate His waiting room with patience, faith, and a sense of peace that only He can provide.

Reflection: How might God be using this waiting season to renew your way of thinking? Are you willing to adopt a mindset of trust, letting go of frustration and surrendering to God's timeline? What could change if you approached waiting with the mind of Christ?

_____

_____

_____

_____

_____

_____

_____

_____

_____

CHARACTER DEVELOPMENT

"And not only that, but we also glory in tribulations, knowing that tribulation produces perseverance; and perseverance, character; and character, hope."
Romans 5:3-4 NKJV

One of the greatest threats to purpose is an undeveloped character. God loves us too much to leave us in a state that could hinder our growth. In His waiting room, He doesn't simply call us to be still; He uses this time as a tool for shaping our character. Just as pressure and time produce a diamond, waiting on God builds the resilience, integrity, and maturity we need to fulfill His calling.

As Romans 5 reminds us, endurance through trials leads to character, and character produces hope. Integrity is a central part of this character transformation. "He who walks with integrity walks securely, but he who perverts his ways will become known" (Proverbs 10:9). Through waiting, God teaches us to walk in alignment with His truth, building a character that stands firm and reflects His faithfulness.

DAY
16

He who walks with integrity walks securely, but he who perverts his ways will become known.
Proverbs 10;9 NKJV

During her years of longing for a child, Hannah faced deep disappointment and heartache. Yet through her waiting, her faith and integrity grew stronger. By the time God blessed her with a son, she was ready not only to receive His promise but to dedicate Samuel back to God.

If you find yourself in God's waiting room, remember that He's using this season to shape a character in you that mirrors His own. God desires our lives to be so refined that what we do and say reflects Him fully, allowing us to walk securely in His purpose.

Reflection: What qualities is God building in you during this waiting season? How can you embrace this time as part of His plan to shape your character?

_____

_____

_____

_____

_____

_____

_____

_____

_____

_____

TRUSTING GOD'S TIMING

"He has made everything beautiful in its time. Also, He has put eternity in their hearts, except that no one can find out the work that God does from beginning to end."
Ecclesiastes 3:11 NKJV

In God's waiting room, one of the greatest lessons we learn is to trust His timing. While we might want answers now, God knows the perfect moment to fulfill His promises. He is never early or late; He acts precisely when His timing will bring the greatest glory to Himself and the greatest good to us.

God's promises are not on our schedule. Just as David waited years to become king and Jesus waited until the right moment to begin His ministry, we too are called to trust that God's timing is perfect. Though it's often difficult, waiting teaches us to surrender our need for control and to trust that God knows best. Remember, He isn't trying to withhold good from you. He wants to give you all that He has promised. He just needs you to trust His timing.

DAY 17

For I know the plans I have for you, declares the Lord, plans for welfare and not for evil, to give you a future and a hope.

Jeremiah 29:11 ESV

Reflection: Is there a situation in your life where you need to trust God's timing? How can you find peace in knowing that God's timing is perfect?

_____

_____

_____

_____

_____

_____

_____

_____

_____

_____

_____

_____

_____

_____

_____

_____

_____

_____

_____

_____

IT'S TIME TO LET IT GO!

"Do not be afraid, for am I in the place of God?
But as for you, you meant evil against me;
but God meant it for good, in order to bring it about
as it is this day, to save many people alive."
Genesis 50:19-20 NKJV

In God's waiting room, letting go of past hurts, failures, and disappointments is often one of the hardest steps to take. Joseph's journey was filled with betrayal, false accusations, and painful trials. Thrown into a pit, sold into slavery, and later falsely imprisoned, Joseph chose not to cling to resentment or bitterness. Each time he faced hardship, he released it to God and moved forward, allowing God to transform his trials into a purpose far greater than he could have imagined.

When Joseph named his sons Manasseh and Ephraim, he recognized that God had not only helped him let go of past struggles but had also blessed him abundantly in the land of his affliction. Joseph's decision to release the pain and forgive those who wronged him positioned him to step into

DAY
18

Forgetting those things which are behind and reaching forward to those things which are ahead. I press toward the goal for the prize of the upward call of God in Christ Jesus.

Philippians 3:13-14 NKJV

God's purpose for his life, ultimately saving his family and countless others.

It's time to let IT go! Holding onto past wounds hinders our growth and blocks the blessings God has prepared for us. God's waiting room is a place of release and renewal. Just as Joseph let go of what was behind him to embrace what lay ahead, we too must release the past to step into God's abundance. Whether it's a hurt, a regret, or a painful memory - whatever "IT" may be, let it go and allow God to transform your waiting season into one of healing and growth.

Reflection: What "IT" do you need to let go of in order to move forward in God's purpose? How might releasing past hurts or disappointments open the door for God's blessings in your life? Is there someone you need to forgive, or a burden you need to release to fully experience the freedom God has for you?

_____

_____

_____

_____

_____

_____

_____

_____

FAITHFUL NOT FAMOUS

"But be sure to fear the Lord and
serve him faithfully with all your heart;
consider what great things he has done for you."
1 Samuel 12:24 NIV

Waiting can feel frustrating, especially when it seems like everyone else is moving forward. Yet, it's often in God's waiting room that He calls us to a deeper faithfulness - a commitment to trust, serve, and honor Him without immediate reward or recognition.

Paul's words in Acts 20:24 remind us that faithfulness isn't about fame or acknowledgment but about completing the course God has set before us with joy and endurance. In the waiting room, our motives are tested, and we learn that our worth isn't tied to achievements but to whom we belong. Faithfulness in this season means trusting God's timing, doing the work He has given us, and knowing that He sees our commitment, even if no one else does.

DAY
19

Through the Lord's mercies we are not consumed, Because His compassions fail not. They are new every morning; Great is Your faithfulness.

Lamentations 3:22-23 NKJV

Consider Job, who remained faithful through devastating loss. He wasn't seeking recognition; he simply trusted God. In the same way, God calls us to be steadfast in our own seasons of waiting, even when it feels unnoticed.

In these quiet moments, we learn to seek God's approval over the applause of others, knowing that His "Well done" is worth far more than worldly recognition. God sees our unseen faithfulness, and being known by Him is far greater than being famous in the eyes of man.

Reflection: Am I more focused on seeking God's approval or on gaining recognition from others during this season of waiting?

_____

_____

_____

_____

_____

_____

_____

_____

_____

_____

_____

THE FRUIT OF THE SPIRIT

"But the fruit of the Spirit is love, joy, peace, longsuffering, kindness, goodness, faithfulness, gentleness, self-control. Against such there is no law."
Galatians 5:22-23 NKJV

Waiting seasons give us the chance to inspect our own hearts. Are we exhibiting the fruit of the Holy Spirit or the works of the flesh? God calls us to let go of self-centered ambitions and embrace His plans for our lives. We are invited to "die" to the works of the flesh, so we may inherit the Kingdom of God (Galatians 5:19-21), and cultivate a heart aligned with Him.

In the waiting room, God is doing more than preparing us for the next season; He is producing fruit that remains. While we may think we're waiting for a specific outcome or answer, God often has a deeper purpose - cultivating within us love, joy, peace, patience, kindness, goodness, faithfulness, gentleness, and self-control. That's why the waiting room can appear in more than one season of our lives. At each stage, God is looking not for the greatness of our gifts but for the presence of His lasting fruit.

DAY
20

Abide in Me, and I in you. As the branch cannot bear fruit of itself, unless it abides in the vine, neither can you, unless you abide in Me.

John 15:4 NKJV

More importantly, please remember that it is not just about the destination, but how you arrive. Let it be with fruit that remains.

Reflection: Ask yourself: Am I allowing God to cultivate the fruit of His Spirit in me during this season of waiting, or am I focused only on reaching the next stage?

_____

_____

_____

_____

_____

_____

_____

_____

_____

_____

_____

_____

_____

_____

_____

_____

_____

Practical Application

1. **Embrace Daily Transformation:** Use this waiting period as a time to invite God's transformative work in your life. Each day, ask Him to reveal areas where He wants to shape your character, increase your faith, and renew your mind. Reflect on Scriptures related to the fruit of the Spirit (Galatians 5:22-23) and actively seek ways to live them out.

2. **Shift Your Thinking to Align with God's Promises**: Waiting can be difficult, but it's an opportunity to replace negative thoughts with God's truth. Spend time each morning focusing on Scriptures that emphasize God's timing, goodness, and faithfulness. Write down any negative thoughts and replace them with affirmations of God's promises, allowing His truth to reshape your thinking.

3. **Let Go and Trust the Process:** Identify areas of your life where you may still be holding on too tightly. Each week, choose one specific area to surrender to God in prayer, asking for His help to trust Him fully.

Affirmation

As I wait on the Lord, I embrace joy, peace, and serenity, trusting in His sovereignty over every situation. I will wait patiently, with eyes to see the deepest needs of others and a heart full of love. My waiting is a time of purpose, focused on serving others and fulfilling His call. I walk in strength and grace, embodying hospitality, and allowing His love to shine through me with humility and compassion.

GUARDING YOUR HEART IN THE WAITING ROOM

Waiting can challenge us on many levels: emotionally, spiritually, and even physically. When God asks us to wait - it can feel like we're standing still while everything around us keeps moving. In these waiting seasons, it's easy for doubt, frustration, and impatience to settle in. Proverbs 4:23 reminds us of something crucial during these times: "Guard your heart, for everything you do flows from it." Just as we protect valuable treasures, we need to protect our hearts from doubt, fear, and negativity.

Our hearts are the wellspring of our lives. Whatever we let take root there - faith or fear, hope or despair - will impact every decision we make, every action we take, and every relationship we build. God invites us to guard our hearts in the waiting room, not as a passive task, but as an active pursuit of His presence, promises, and peace.

DAY 21

Keep your heart with all diligence,
For out of it spring the issues of life.
Proverbs 4:23 NKJV

Reflection: How can you actively guard your heart against doubt, frustration, or impatience in this season of waiting, and what practices can help you stay focused on God's promises?

_____

_____

_____

_____

_____

_____

_____

_____

_____

_____

_____

_____

_____

_____

_____

_____

_____

_____

_____

THINK ON THESE THINGS

"Set your mind on things above, not on earthly things."
Colossians 3:2 NIV

When we're in a season of waiting, it's all too easy to let our hearts become heavy with "what ifs" and "whys." We replay scenarios in our minds, dwell on missed opportunities, and sometimes wonder if God has forgotten about us. These thoughts can weigh us down and cloud our vision, distracting us from recognizing what God is actively doing within us. That's why it's essential to guard our hearts by setting our minds on things above, as Colossians 3:2 encourages.

Guarding your heart isn't just about keeping negative things out - it's about filling it with the right things. Philippians 4:8 tells us to think on things that are true, noble, and praiseworthy. When doubt creeps in, we must turn to God's Word, allowing His promises to clear away the fog of uncertainty and light our path. We must actively choose to focus on God's faithfulness When we meditate on these things, we invite God's peace to guard our hearts, renewing our strength and keeping us anchored in hope.

DAY

22

You will keep him in perfect peace,
Whose mind is stayed on You,
Because he trusts in You.
Isaiah 26:3 NKJV

Reflection: What "what ifs" or "whys" have been clouding your thoughts lately? How can you intentionally replace those worries with the truths found in God's Word? What scriptures can you focus on this week to keep your mind set on the things above?

_____

_____

_____

_____

_____

_____

_____

_____

_____

_____

_____

_____

_____

_____

_____

_____

_____

_____

_____

PRAY HONESTLY

"Be anxious for nothing, but in everything by prayer
and supplication, with thanksgiving, let your requests be
made known to God; and the peace of God, which
surpasses all understanding, will guard your
hearts and minds through Christ Jesus."
Philippians 4:6-7 NKJV

In difficult seasons, it's easy to feel like you have to put on a brave face or handle things on your own. But God invites us to bring our true selves to Him in prayer. Honest and consistent prayer keeps us connected to God's heart, allowing Him to pour strength and peace into us.

In these vulnerable moments with God, we open our hearts fully to His presence. By bringing everything to Him in prayer, we allow Him to lift the weight of our anxieties, renewing us with His peace. He wants to walk with us through every emotion and give us the endurance we need. When we share our hearts with God, He works on our behalf, turning our concerns into places of growth and trust.

DAY
23

*Men always ought to pray and
not lose heart.*
Luke 18:1 NKJV

Reflection: What emotions have you been holding back from God in this season? How can praying honestly strengthen your relationship with Him? What would it look like to develop a habit of sharing everything with God, even the things that feel hard to admit?

_____

_____

_____

_____

_____

_____

_____

_____

_____

_____

_____

_____

_____

_____

_____

_____

_____

_____

_____

_____

ENCOURAGING YOURSELF

"Be of good courage, and He shall strengthen your heart,
All you who hope in the Lord.
Psalm 31:24 NKJV

Encouragement is important, especially in difficult times. Surrounding yourself with a supportive community and drawing strength from God's Word are two powerful ways to stay uplifted. Hebrews 10:24-25 urges us to "spur one another on toward love and good deeds" and to meet together, while 1 Thessalonians 5:11 instructs us to "encourage one another and build each other up." Healthy relationships can remind us of God's faithfulness and provide needed perspective and prayer.

When you find yourself without supportive voices nearby, encourage yourself in the Lord. Lean into God's Word and speak His promises over your life. Psalm 24:7-10 declares God's power and might, reminding us that He is the King of Glory, strong and mighty in battle. His Word provides unshakeable assurance that He is always with you and will carry you through.

DAY 24

"Lift up your heads, O you gates! And be lifted up, you everlasting doors! And the King of glory shall come in.

Psalm 24:7 NKJV

Reflection: Who are the people in your life who encourage you in your faith journey? How can you cultivate the habit of encouraging yourself in the Lord when you're alone? Are there Scriptures you can focus on to keep your heart encouraged in any season?

_____

_____

_____

_____

_____

_____

_____

_____

_____

_____

_____

_____

_____

_____

_____

_____

_____

_____

_____

Practical Application

1. **Set Your Mind on God's Truth:** When waiting feels overwhelming, take intentional steps to focus on God's Word. Each day, write down one encouraging truth from Scripture to help you stay centered on God's faithfulness and goodness.

2. **Create a Daily Prayer Routine**: Make prayer a consistent part of your day, setting aside specific times to be honest with God about your fears, hopes, and frustrations. Let this be a time to listen as well, allowing God's peace to fill your heart as you trust Him with each part of your journey.

3. **Build a "Spiritual Encouragement Toolkit":** Surround yourself with reminders of God's promises: keep uplifting Scriptures, worship songs, or messages that bring hope readily accessible. When encouragement isn't coming from those around you, turn to this toolkit and actively speak God's promises over your life.

Affirmation

Today, I guard my heart and mind, focusing on what is above and rejecting negative influences. I put on the armor of God, strapping on the belt of truth and the breastplate of righteousness to protect my heart. God is my defender and protector, filling me with His love, peace, and strength. I walk with confidence, guided by His presence and aligning my words and thoughts with His truth.

QUITTING IS NOT AN OPTION

Life will test us, often in ways we never expected. Challenges come in many forms - work gets hard, relationships become strained, dreams feel distant, and sometimes it seems easier to just give up. But quitting is not an option when we understand that there is a purpose in everything we endure. God's Word reminds us that our work has a reward if we stand firm.

Think about this: what are you on the verge of quitting? Is it your marriage, your job, your dream, or even your faith? Maybe it's because the journey feels too hard, the results seem too slow, or you're facing criticism and discouragement from others. But God has placed greatness within you. He has given you strength and potential, and each one of us has a unique purpose designed by Him.

DAY 25

But as for you, be strong; don't give up,
for your work has a reward.
2 Chronicles 15:7 NKJV

Reflection: Have you felt tempted to quit during this waiting season? What goals has God placed in your heart that require perseverance and faith? How can you remind yourself daily that quitting is not an option, no matter how tough the waiting becomes?

_____

_____

_____

_____

_____

_____

_____

_____

_____

_____

_____

_____

_____

_____

_____

_____

_____

_____

_____

FACING YOUR FEARS

"For God has not given us a spirit of fear, but of power and
of love and of a sound mind."
2 Timothy 1:7 NKJV

Fear is a powerful emotion, and when it takes hold, it can paralyze us, stopping us in our tracks. Fear whispers lies - "You're not good enough," "What if you fail?" "You're alone in this." But God's Word reminds us that fear does not come from Him. 2 Timothy 1:7 assures us that God has not given us a spirit of fear but of power, love, and a sound mind. When fear tries to weaken our resolve, we have God's promise that He is with us.

With God's help, we can confront the fears that try to hold us back. He is not only with us; He is within us, and His power is greater than anything that stands in our way (1 John 4:4). Even in the face of overwhelming challenges, God gives us the courage to keep moving forward, knowing that "with God, nothing will be impossible" (Luke 1:37).

DAY
26

I sought the Lord, and He heard me,
And delivered me from all my fears.
Psalm 34:4 NKJV

91

Reflection: What fears may be keeping you from stepping into God's purpose for you? How can you remind yourself of God's power within you when fear tries to creep in? Are there specific Scriptures or promises from God that help you strengthen your faith in times of fear?

_____

_____

_____

_____

_____

_____

_____

_____

_____

_____

_____

_____

_____

_____

_____

_____

_____

_____

_____

THIS THING

"Concerning this thing I pleaded with the Lord three times
that it might depart from me."
2 Corinthians 12:8 NKJV

Sometimes, life hands us a "thing" - a burden, a thorn, a
weakness - that feels insurmountable. For Paul, it was a
"thorn in the flesh." He prayed three times for it to be
removed, but God's answer was not what he expected.
Instead of deliverance, God promised His grace. Just like
Paul, we may have a "thing" that we didn't ask for, a
challenge or limitation that feels unfair or unbearable. But
this "thing" is often God's way of keeping us humble,
reminding us of His strength working in us.

Consider your own "thing"- perhaps a struggle you didn't
see coming, something that causes embarrassment or even
shame. It may be physical, emotional, or relational. This
challenge might feel like a barrier to your calling, but God
sees it as an opportunity to display His strength in your life.

When we lean into His grace, refusing to quit, we experience

DAY

27

*Therefore I take pleasure in infirmities, in
reproaches, in needs, in persecutions, in
distresses, for Christ's sake. For when I am
weak, then I am strong.*
2 Corinthians 12:10 NKJV

a deeper reliance on Him and a strength we cannot find on our own.

Reflecting on my own story, I know what it's like to carry a physical limitation that humbles me daily. I've asked God to take it away, because I can't fix it, and yet His answer remains the same: "My grace is sufficient for you." I'm learning, just as Paul did, that this thorn is not a reason to quit. Instead, it's a call to depend on God more fully and let His power rest on me, even when I feel weak. Embracing this "thing" is a reminder that, with God, I can keep moving forward, trusting that His grace will sustain me every step of the way.

Reflection: What is your "thing" - the weakness or limitation you wish you could change or remove? How might God be using this "thing" to draw you closer to Him and show His strength in your life? Are you willing to trust God's grace as sufficient, even if the "thing" remains?

_____

_____

_____

_____

_____

_____

_____

_____

WHEN IT GETS HARD

"The Lord will perfect that which concerns me;
Your mercy, O Lord, endures forever; Do not forsake the
works of Your hands."
Psalm 138:8 NKJV

The journey to fulfilling God's purpose can be challenging. It's hard when doors close, when others criticize or misunderstand us, when we're exhausted, or when we don't see immediate results. In these moments, think of a seed that has been buried in the ground. Hidden beneath the soil, it appears as though nothing is happening. But in that unseen place, the seed is breaking open, taking root, and beginning to grow. Though growth is invisible at first, soon it will push through the soil and begin to flourish.

In the same way, God is working within you during this process. Psalm 138:8 reassures us that "The Lord will perfect that which concerns me." This is not the time to quit. You're being molded and shaped for His purpose, and He will not forsake the work of His hands. God will fulfill what He has promised.

DAY

28

Be merciful to me, O God, be merciful to me! For my soul trusts in You; And in the shadow of Your wings I will make my refuge, Until these calamities have passed by.

Psalm 57:1 NKJV

97

Reflection: In moments when the journey feels especially tough, what reminders or truths about God's faithfulness can help you keep moving forward?

_____

_____

_____

_____

_____

_____

_____

_____

_____

_____

_____

_____

_____

_____

_____

_____

_____

_____

_____

_____

_____

I'M COMING OUT OF THIS

"The righteous cry out, and the Lord hears,
And delivers them out of all their troubles."
Psalm 34:17 NKJV

Romans 5 teaches us something profound: our tribulations aren't pointless; they're producing something greater within us. Through struggles, God is developing our perseverance, refining our character, and anchoring us in a hope that doesn't disappoint. This hope isn't a vague optimism - it's a confident expectation rooted in God's promises and the unfailing love poured out in our hearts by the Holy Spirit.

In seasons of hardship, it's easy to feel overwhelmed or to question why we're facing certain challenges. Yet God, who sees the beginning from the end, is using every struggle to build spiritual resilience in us. Just as silver and gold are refined through fire, God uses trials to purify our hearts and strengthen our faith. Each challenge we endure isn't the end - it's part of God's refining process, a path toward a deeper relationship with Him. Be assured, God is with you and will deliver you. You're coming out of this!

DAY
29

You are my hiding place; You shall preserve me from trouble; You shall surround me with songs of deliverance. Selah.

Psalm 32:7 NKJV

Reflection: How has God used a past struggle to build strength, resilience, or deeper faith in you? Where might He be doing this in your life right now?

_____

_____

_____

_____

_____

_____

_____

_____

_____

_____

_____

_____

_____

_____

_____

_____

_____

_____

TEMPORARY STRUGGLES

"For our light affliction, which is but for a moment,
is working for us a far more exceeding and eternal
weight of glory…"
2 Corinthians 4:17 NKJV

Quitting isn't just about walking away from a task; it's about turning from the purpose God has for you. When we're in the midst of struggles, it's easy to feel discouraged, wondering if it's worth pressing on. But God reminds us that these difficulties are temporary and that He is using them to shape us for something far greater. These "light afflictions" may feel heavy now, but they are building an eternal glory that far outweighs the pain we're experiencing.

Temporary setbacks, as painful as they are, can be stepping stones toward a more powerful, purpose-driven life. Don't let today's challenges rob you of the tomorrow God has prepared for you. Trust in His process, stand firm in faith, and remember that the future He has planned is worth every struggle you may be facing now.

DAY
30

But may the God of all grace, who called
us to His eternal glory by Christ Jesus,
after you have suffered a while, perfect,
establish, strengthen, and settle you.

1 Peter 5:10 NKJV

Reflection: How might God be using your current challenges to shape you for His greater purpose, and what steps can you take to trust His process instead of giving up?

_____

_____

_____

_____

_____

_____

_____

_____

_____

_____

_____

_____

_____

_____

_____

_____

_____

_____

_____

Practical Application

1. **Reconnect with Your Purpose**: Reflect on why you started and write down the original vision or calling that brought you to this point. Keep it visible to remind yourself of the bigger picture God has for you.

2. **Seek Strength Through Prayer and Scripture**: Commit to daily prayer, asking God for the strength to persevere. Memorize key scriptures like Philippians 4:13 or Isaiah 41:10 to reinforce your faith when challenges arise.

3. **Surround Yourself with Support**: Connect with trusted friends or mentors who encourage your journey. Share your progress with them and lean on their support to stay focused and motivated.

Affirmation

Quitting is not an option. I will not quit on God. I trust Him fully and will never let Him go. He holds me and will never leave nor forsake me. I choose to remain steadfast in Him. I stand firm on His promises, knowing His Word will produce fruit in every area of my life.

IT IS NOT TOO LATE TO BEGIN AGAIN!

Starting over often stirs a mix of fear and excitement. When we think about beginning again, we may worry about past mistakes, the opinions of others, or the possibility of failure. But God is a God of new beginnings, offering us fresh opportunities to begin again - no matter how many times we've stumbled or fallen.

The Bible assures us that God is always ready to lead us into a new season. Isaiah 43:18-19 tells us to let go of the past and embrace the new thing God is doing. When God calls us to begin again, it's not about erasing our history but about stepping into a future shaped by His grace and filled with purpose. Each new beginning is an opportunity for growth, renewal, and deeper dependence on Him.

DAY 31

Therefore, if anyone is in Christ, he is a new creation; old things have passed away; behold, all things have become new.

2 Corinthians 5:17

107

In life, new beginnings can come in various forms and seasons. They may involve a career change, a new relationship, or a renewed commitment to spiritual growth. Whatever it is, God grants us these fresh starts to refine us and bring us closer to His purpose. Ecclesiastes 7:8 reminds us, "The end of a thing is better than its beginning." No matter how our journey started, God assures us that He has a powerful, fulfilling end in mind.

Embracing a new beginning also means letting go of the past. We are called to move beyond former failures, regrets, or even successes. God offers a clean slate, inviting us to trust in His guidance as He makes a way in the wilderness and brings life to what once felt barren. Our journey will have its ups and downs, but with perseverance, we will see His promises unfold.

Reflection: Are there areas in your life where God is inviting you to begin again? How can you let go of past mistakes or doubts and trust God's plan for a fresh start? What steps can you take today to embrace this new season with faith and perseverance?

PIVOT FOR PURPOSE

"I will arise and go to my Father…"
Luke 15:18 NKJV

There are moments when we find ourselves at a crossroads; perhaps you've walked away from a calling, a relationship, or a pursuit that once felt important to you. The beauty of God's grace is that it allows us to begin again, no matter how many times we've stopped or fallen short. His purpose for your life doesn't end because of a setback or a season of quitting. Instead, He invites you to pivot, refocus, and step boldly into the life He's prepared for you.

Think of the Prodigal Son, who found himself at his lowest, in a pigpen. He had hit rock bottom, but he didn't stay there. Remembering who he was and who his father was, he got up and went back home. That moment became a turning point toward restoration.

The Bible offers powerful examples of people who pivoted and received fresh starts with renewed purpose. Saul, who

DAY
32

And He said, "Your name shall no longer be called Jacob, but Israel: for you have struggled with God and with men, and have prevailed."

Genesis 32:28 NKJV

once persecuted Christians, encountered Jesus and pivoted from his old life to become the Apostle Paul - one of the most influential ambassadors of Christ. Abram, who had already begun a journey in faith, received a new purpose and a new name, Abraham, as a sign of his covenant with God. Jacob, wrestling with his past and with God, refused to let go until he received his blessing, becoming Israel and stepping into his destiny.

If you feel you've quit or turned away from something God placed in your heart, remember that He specializes in new beginnings. Your past mistakes don't disqualify you. The key is to pivot - turn away from - and align yourself with God's purpose. Quitting doesn't have to be the end; it can be a pause before a powerful renewal.

Reflection: Is there an area in your life where God is inviting you to pivot, to realign with His purpose and step back into what He has called you to do? What past setbacks or doubts do you need to release to fully embrace the new beginning God is offering you?

_____

_____

_____

_____

_____

_____

YOU ARE STILL DESTINED

"For the vision is yet for an appointed time; But at the end it will speak, and it will not lie. Though it tarries, wait for it; Because it will surely come, It will not tarry."
Habakkuk 2:3 NKJV

Have you ever felt like God's promises for your life were delayed? Maybe He placed a vision in your heart, yet everything around you seems to be moving in the opposite direction. Life's detours can leave us questioning if we misunderstood His plans or if we're still on the path He intended. But here's the truth: even when delayed, you are still destined.

Consider Joseph's journey. God gave him a vision of leadership, but the years following looked nothing like what he envisioned. Betrayed by his brothers, sold into slavery, falsely accused, and thrown into prison - Joseph faced setback after setback. Despite his circumstances, he held onto God's promises and trusted that his destiny was still in God's hands.

DAY

33

Your promises have been thoroughly tested, and your servant loves them.
Psalm 119:140 NIV

If God has given you a vision, remember that He's already seen the end from the beginning. The delays you face aren't denials. In His timing, everything will come together, and the promise He gave you will manifest. Believe for it!

Reflection: Do you believe that you are still destined for God's purpose, even when your circumstances seem to say otherwise? Are you trusting God's timing for His promises, or are you letting delays discourage your faith in the vision He placed in your heart?

IT'S TIME FOR A RESET

"I am the vine; you are the branches. If you remain in me
and I in you, you will bear much fruit; apart from me you
can do nothing."
John 15:5 NIV

Sometimes we find ourselves needing a reset, having
become disconnected from the true source of our strength,
purpose, and joy. Just as a branch must stay connected to the
vine to thrive, our lives require continual reconnection to
Christ. As John 15:5 reminds us, He is the vine and we are
the branches; apart from Him, we can do nothing. Without a
reset, we may find ourselves trying to live in our own
strength, wondering why life feels stagnant or disconnected.

When an appliance malfunctions, the GFCI switch may trip,
signaling a disconnect. In the same way, our spiritual lives
may "trip" when weighed down by life, distractions,
unconfessed sins, or old habits that drain us. God's Spirit
nudges us to reset and reconnect to the source of true life -
Christ Himself, the vine that sustains and empowers us.

DAY
34

*But those who wait on the Lord shall renew
their strength; They shall mount up with
wings like eagles, They shall run and not
be weary, They shall walk and not faint.*

Isaiah 40:31 NKJV

If God is calling you to reset and reconnect, now is the time. No matter where you've been or what has happened, it's never too late to begin again. Trust Him to lead you into a new season, fill you with His strength, guide you by His Spirit, and prepare you for the new work He is ready to do in your life!

Reflection: Is there an area in your life where God might be inviting you to reset and reconnect? Are you open to the new work God wants to do in your life, even if it requires a reset in your priorities or mindset?

_____

_____

_____

_____

_____

_____

_____

_____

_____

_____

_____

_____

IT'S TIME TO GET UP

"Don't interfere with good people's lives; don't try to get the best of them. No matter how many times you trip them up, God-loyal people don't stay down long; soon they're up on their feet, while the wicked end up flat on their faces."
Proverbs 24:16 MSG

Life will inevitably bring setbacks - moments when we stumble, face challenges, or experience failure. But Proverbs 24:16 reminds us of a powerful truth: no matter how many times a godly person is knocked down, they will rise again. You may have faced adversity, disappointments, or attacks from the enemy, but you were never meant to stay down. God has placed His strength within you, and because of that, you will rise.

You will rise from the ashes, from past mistakes, and from any fall. The enemy may try to trip you up, but God's Spirit within you gives you the power to get back on your feet and move forward in His purpose. If you've been knocked down, let today be your turning point. It's time to get up! The past

DAY
35

You are of God, little children, and have overcome them, because He who is in you is greater than he who is in the world.

1 John 4:4 NKJV

is behind you, and though you may have experienced failures, they do not define you. Let go, embrace God's forgiveness, and walk forward with strength and courage.

As His child, it's in you to rise - because He is in you. No more lingering in negative thoughts that hold you back. God's purpose is still alive in you, and the world needs what He has placed in your life. It's time to get up, take your rightful place, and step forward. There is work to do and lives to transform, all for His glory.

Reflection: What areas in your life have you allowed past setbacks or failures to keep you down? What steps can you take today to "get up" and embrace the new opportunities and purposes God has for you?

_____

_____

_____

_____

_____

_____

_____

_____

_____

_____

Practical Application

1. **Reflect and Release:** Take time to identify any past setbacks, regrets, or negative thoughts that may be holding you back. Pray and release these to God, asking for His help to let go and embrace a fresh start. Remember, beginning again requires freeing yourself from what's behind to fully step into what's ahead.

2. **Realign with God's Purpose**: Spend intentional time in prayer and God's Word to reconnect with His vision for your life. Ask Him to reveal areas where you may need a pivot or reset. Seek His guidance to confirm your direction and to empower you to step forward with renewed clarity and courage.

3. **Take a Small Step Forward**: Begin today by taking one small, practical step toward the life and purpose God has called you to.

Affirmation

Today, I choose to begin again, forgetting the past and focusing on the dreams and visions ahead. I will fight for my family, deepen my relationship with God, and move forward without fear or discouragement. God strengthens and helps me, upholding me with His righteous hand. Delayed but still destined, I stand in faith to receive His promises.

WHAT THE EYE DID NOT SEE

Sometimes, what God is doing in our lives goes unnoticed because it's happening just below the surface. We wait, pray, and hope for growth, yet nothing seems to change. But 1 Corinthians 2:9 reminds us that God has unimaginable plans for us, things no eye has seen and no ear has heard. Often, His greatest work is hidden from view, preparing us for a future that far exceeds our expectations.

Consider the bamboo tree. For years, it appears as though nothing is happening. Day after day, there is no visible sign of growth above the surface. But during that time, the bamboo's roots are spreading wide and deep, creating a foundation capable of sustaining its eventual growth. Then, in just a few short weeks, the bamboo can shoot up as much as 90 feet. The sudden growth

DAY
36

But as it is written: "Eye has not seen, nor ear heard, nor have entered into the heart of man the things which God has prepared for those who love Him.
1 Corinthians 2:9 NKJV

we see above ground is only possible because of the years spent building strength and stability beneath the soil.

In the same way, God's work in us is often hidden from sight. We may feel like we're standing still, wondering if anything is really happening. But beneath the surface, God is fortifying our character, deepening our faith, and increasing our trust in Him. The unseen process is essential for the visible promise. When the time is right, the growth will be rapid and evident, but only because of the foundational work He has done within us.

Reflection: What areas of growth or preparation might God be working on beneath the surface of your life that you haven't noticed? How can you begin to recognize and appreciate His hidden work during this season?

_____

_____

_____

_____

_____

_____

_____

_____

_____

_____

YOU'RE NEXT IN LINE

"Then God remembered Rachel, and God listened to her
and opened her womb."
Genesis 30:22 NKJV

Have you ever sat in a hospital waiting room, watching others being called back to be seen or discharged before you? It's tempting to think, "Did they forget about me? Why am I still waiting?" Sometimes, we only see others moving forward and wonder when our turn will come. But here's the truth: you are next in line! God has not forgotten you or left you behind. You're not overlooked; you're simply waiting for the right moment - your moment.

God knows exactly when and how to bring His promises to fruition in your life. Each blessing and breakthrough He has for you is custom-made, waiting for the right time to unfold. While you wait, know that He is working to bring about something greater than you can imagine. Just as God remembered Rachel in Genesis 30, He remembers you too. Your waiting is not in vain. Celebrate in faith! You're next!

DAY 37

And let us not grow weary while doing good, for in due season we shall reap if we do not lose heart.

Galatians 6:9 NKJV

Reflection: How does knowing you're next in line bring you hope and excitement for what God has prepared?

_____

_____

_____

_____

_____

_____

_____

_____

_____

_____

_____

_____

_____

_____

_____

_____

_____

_____

_____

GOD WAS THERE ALL ALONG

"Be strong and of good courage, do not fear nor be afraid
of them; for the Lord your God, He is the One who goes
with you. He will not leave you nor forsake you."
Deuteronomy 31:6 NKJV

Throughout every step of your journey, God has been right
there, faithfully by your side. He was with you when He first
gave you the promise, He was with you in the waiting, and
He'll be with you when you receive it. At no point did God
ever leave you alone. Even when the path seemed unclear or
difficult, He was present, working in ways that may not have
been visible to you but were no less powerful.

You may not have always seen His hand, but He was there -
- providing in unexpected ways, sending encouragement
through strangers, and assigning angels to protect you. Every
prayer you whispered, He heard. When you were too tired to
walk, He carried you; when you were weak, He strengthened
you; when you cried, He comforted you. God has been there
at every turn, holding you, fighting for you, and loving you
through it all.

DAY

38

The Lord has appeared of old to me,
saying: "Yes, I have loved you with an
everlasting love; Therefore with
lovingkindness I have drawn you.

Jeremiah 31:3 NKJV

129

Reflection: Can you look back and see moments when God was present, even if you didn't recognize it at the time? How does knowing that God will never leave or forsake you give you confidence for the future?

_____

_____

_____

_____

_____

_____

_____

_____

_____

_____

_____

_____

_____

_____

_____

_____

_____

_____

_____

_____

_____

THE PROMISE FULFILLED

"And you know in all your hearts and in all your souls that not one thing has failed of all the good things which the Lord your God spoke concerning you. All have come to pass for you; not one word of them has failed."

Joshua 23:14 NKJV

As Joshua reminded the Israelites, "not one thing has failed of all the good things which the Lord your God spoke concerning you." God's promises were fulfilled exactly as He had said. Every stage of their journey - the beginning, the middle, and the end - was essential in bringing God's promise to completion. Similarly, in our lives, each step of the journey is part of the promise.

Think about baking a cake. When you gather the ingredients, you have everything needed, but it's not yet in its final form. Flour, sugar, eggs, and other ingredients are combined, but the process doesn't stop there. The batter must be mixed, poured into a pan, and baked at the right temperature for a specific time. Each stage is necessary to produce the final result. In the same way, each phase of your journey is like an

DAY
39

Therefore know that the Lord your God, He is God, the faithful God who keeps covenant and mercy for a thousand generations with those who love Him and keep His commandments...

Deuteronomy 7:9 NKJV

ingredient God is using to fulfill His promise in your life. What might feel like waiting or working toward the promise is actually part of living it - step by step, with each moment contributing to the fulfillment of what He has spoken over you.

Wherever you are in your journey, remember that you're not just waiting to "arrive" at the promise. You are walking in it, and God is actively bringing everything together to complete it in His perfect time. The process may still be unfolding, but each experience, challenge, and victory is a vital part of the promise coming to life. Embrace where you are with confidence, knowing that you are already living in the promise, and God is weaving every part together beautifully for His glory.

Reflection: In what ways might God already be fulfilling His promise in your life, even if the outcome isn't fully visible yet? How can you embrace your current stage in the journey, seeing it as a vital part of the promise?

_____

_____

_____

_____

_____

_____

Practical Application

1. **Reflect on God's Presence and Faithfulness**: Spend time in reflection or journaling to identify moments when you may not have fully recognized God's presence or provision in your journey. Consider how He may have been working behind the scenes to prepare and protect you, even if it wasn't visible at the time. This exercise can deepen your awareness of His ongoing faithfulness.

2. **Renew Your Trust in God's Timing:** When you find yourself anxious or doubtful, reaffirm your trust in God's perfect timing. Pray and remind yourself that you are "next in line" for what He has promised. This can help you stay grounded in faith, rather than feeling discouraged by delays.

3. **Actively Prepare for the Fulfillment of His Promises**: While waiting, take practical steps to prepare yourself for the promises you're expecting. Actively preparing demonstrates trust that His promise is coming and readiness to step fully into it when it arrives.

Affirmation

My foundation is solid, even when I can't see it. I am being developed for greatness and built to endure all seasons. I release anything holding me back and make room for growth, knowing that even when results aren't immediate, progress is happening. I refuse to be discouraged by what I can't yet see because I am being strengthened and prepared for something bigger and better.

MADE IN THE MIDDLE

Prayerfully, you now see that it's in the middle where both you and God's promises for you are truly made. Not at the beginning, when the vision is fresh and clear, and not at the end, when the promise is fully visible and fulfilled. It's in the middle - through the process itself - that we're shaped and refined, growing stronger and more deeply rooted in our faith.

The middle is where God brings together all the elements of His work in your life. It's where He strengthens your character, teaches you endurance, and deepens your trust in Him. Every struggle, every victory, and every moment in between is part of His divine process. The middle isn't a detour; it's the main route on the road to His promise. It's where the promise takes shape and where you're molded into the person who can fully receive it.

DAY

40

Being confident of this very thing, that He who has begun a good work in you will complete it until the day of Jesus Christ.
Philippians 1:6 NKJV

May you never see the middle as an inconvenience or disruption again. Instead, embrace this stage as the path God has designed for you - not just to reach the promise, but to become all He has purposed you to be.

The middle is filled with opportunities to witness God's miracles, to discover promises within the promise, and to experience His faithfulness in real, tangible ways. God is ever-present with you, sustaining you, guiding you, and ensuring that you don't have to fear failing, because He holds you. He knows exactly what He's doing and is completing His work in you, moment by moment. You are being prepared and strengthened for what lies ahead, made ready to carry the fullness of His promise.

As you close this journey through *Made in the Middle*, remember that God is with you in every stage. The beginning may spark hope, and the end may bring joy, but it's in the middle where faith grows deep, promises unfold, and transformation occurs. You are not just on the way to the promise - you're living in it, one step at a time. Embrace the middle with gratitude, knowing that "He who has begun a good work in you will complete it until the day of Jesus Christ" (Philippians 1:6 NKJV).

Reflection: As you look back over these 40 days, how has your perspective on the 'middle' seasons of life changed? In what ways do you feel God has been shaping and preparing you through this journey, and how can you embrace His work in your life as you continue forward?

_____

_____

_____

_____

_____

_____

_____

_____

_____

_____

_____

_____

_____

_____

_____

_____

_____

_____

_____

"

I'm not intimidated by what others don't see; I'm motivated by what's within me. My next move is my best move.

Myraio L. Mitchell, Sr.